TO THE CYPRESS AGAIN AND AGAIN:
TRIBUTE TO SALVADOR ESPRIU

Praise for TO THE CYPRESS AGAIN AND AGAIN:
TRIBUTE TO SALVADOR ESPRIU

"At this particular darkening hour in Europe, we are graced by Cyrus Cassells's homage to Salvador Espriu. A survivor of Spain's civil war, who then became an internal émigré, Espriu knew intimately the cost of war and destruction. In exquisite, moving poems such as *Sinera Cemetery*, masterfully rendered by Cassells, we encounter Espriu's grieved, but resolute, fortitude: 'Liberty, the enduring word I utter time and again/between ancient boundaries/of vineyards and the sea.' Cassells's dialogue with Espriu is a gift, an enactment of the sacred pledge to uphold, against all odds, the 'enduring word.'"

—Ellen Hinsey, author of *The Illegal Age* and *Update on the Descent*

"*To the Cypress Again and Again: Tribute to Salvador Espriu* is a triumph of affinities, a testament to a translator's steady, slow-burning attention to a poet's work—and to the rich metamorphoses sparked by such devotion. These charged, luminous translations exalt Espriu's stark lyrics; not just accompanying but also communicating with them, Cassells's own poems are contemplative and ecstatic. Every translation is a conversation, and I'm grateful for this book as an example of both how and why."

—Robin Myers, translator of *Copy* by Dolores Dorantes
and *Another Life* by Daniel Lipara

TO THE CYPRESS AGAIN AND AGAIN:
TRIBUTE TO SALVADOR ESPRIU

translated from the Catalan
by Cyrus Cassells

STEPHEN F. AUSTIN STATE UNIVERSITY PRESS

ISBN: 978-1-62288-942-6

For more information: Stephen F. Austin State University Press
P.O. Box 13007 SFA Station
Nacogdoches, Texas 75962
936-468-1078

Distributed by Texas A&M University Press Consortium
www.tamupress.com

In memory of Salvador Espriu

1913–1985

When I grow too old in my mighty effort
to pass a plow through all my memories...

In memory of Helen Joan Freeman

1931–2003

Blessed be

THIS BOOK IS FOR ÀLEX SUSANNA
AND FRANCESC PARCERISAS

ah, joves llavis desclosos despres
de la foscor...

CONTENTS

III. For The Catalan Keeper of the Flame: Poems Inspired by Espriu

ACKNOWLEDGMENTS

These translations and poems have appeared in the following journals, some in earlier versions:

Arkansas International: "Song of Twilight"
Callaloo: "To The Cypress Again and Again"
Neck: "Book of the Dead," "Garden of Five Trees," and "Tree"
Nine Mile: Sinera Cemetery (thirty-part sequence), "Two Poets Quarreling under the Jacarandas"
Passengers Journal: "Song of Triumphant Night," "After the Trees"
The Taos Journal of International Poetry and Art: "Black Land"
Translation (The Journal of Literary Translation): "After The Trees," "Autumn," "From the Theater Itself," "Memory,""Possible Introduction to an Epithalamium," "Sinera Cemetery" (single poem), *Sinera Cemetery* (parts I, IV, XIX, XX, XXI)
Verse Daily: "More Than Peace and Cypresses"

"To The Cypress Again and Again" appears in my second volume, *Soul Make a Path through Shouting;* "More than Peace and Cypresses" in my fourth volume of the same name; and "Two Poets Quarreling under the Jacarandas" appears in my sixth volume, *The Gospel according to Wild Indigo.*

Many thanks to the late Jaume Vidal Alcover, Margo Berdeshevsky, Magda Bogin, Elena Karina Byrne, Randall Couch, Dídac Llorens-Cubedo (especially for his marvelous, discerning essay, "The Voice of the Cypresses: Cyrus Cassells and The Poetry of Salvador Espriu"), Sharon Dolin, John Felstiner, Veronica Golos, Guillem-Jordi Graells, Sara Henning, Robin Myers, Mary Ann Newman, Francesc Parcerisas, the late David H. Rosenthal, Misia Sert, Lisa Russ Spaar for permission to quote from her review of *Still Life with Children: Selected Poems of Francesc Parcerisas*, Alèx Susanna, Kimberly Verhines, Emily Young, and *Institut Ramon Llull* for its stalwart support over the years.

I. A HOMELAND SO SMALL I DREAM OF IT WHOLE

In my country of Vallès
three hills equal a mountain
four pines a cluttered wood
five towns too colossal a world.

*

A hope toppled,
an everlasting regret.
And a homeland so small
I dream of it whole.

—Pere Quart, "Songs of Exile"

"Have pity on the man who moves deeper and deeper,
past any hope of return, into the prisons of yearning
and of years gone by."

— Espriu, *Esther's First Story*

Cypresses in Sinera Cemetery (photo by Cyrus Cassells, 2018)

INTRODUCTION: A HOMELAND SO SMALL
I DREAM OF IT WHOLE

There are some trees on this round earth so riveting, so giant, rooted, and commanding, it's as if the Greek pantheon had taken green form; the cypresses leading up to the hilltop cemetery in Arenys de Mar are just such Olympian trees. Impressive titans, they usher a visitor to the graves' marble stillness and the butter-yellow chapel. In this green-guarded walkway, it's possible to cast your eye through the arched gate with its unassuming cross, past the sheltering cypresses, and detect only the Mediterranean's teal swatch—as if the graveyard opened magically onto water. It's here, where a marine beauty is serenely braided with a staunch reverence for the past, that Salvador Espriu (1913-1985) came, in the Spanish Civil War's crushing aftermath, to mourn the dead and to decry the muzzling of Catalan culture.

Before the war's ferocious free-fall and the Spanish Republic's collapse, Espriu had been a prolific literary prodigy, with five books to his name, two novels and three short story collections: *El doctor Rip* (*Doctor Rip*, 1931), *Laia* (1932), *Aspectes* (1934), *Ariadna al laberint grotesc* (*Ariadne in the Grotesque Labyrinth*, 1935), and *Miratge a Citerea* (*Mirage at Citerea*, 1935). These early works of fiction are marked by dazzling stylistic and linguistic exploration and filtered through a decidedly ironic or satirical lens. As a result of Franco's military conquest and tyrannical banning of the Catalan language ("Don't bark! Speak the language of the empire!"), Espriu turned almost exclusively to poetry and plays. As he struggled to preserve his imperiled language and patrimony ("we learned to descend / steps of grief, / my people and I"), his poems achieved a spare intensity and a meticulous, bare-bones beauty, reminiscent of Samuel Beckett. According to Catalan critic Dídac Llorens-Cubedo, "Espriu produced a body of literature that can be considered, among other things, a vindication of his own language, persecuted and belittled under Franco's regime."

The novelist Maria Aurèlia Capmany (1918-1991), a steadfast friend of Espriu, insisted the poet's piercing civil war experience "rendered his ideal of harmony in political difference and cultural diversity in Spain dramatically impossible and, at a personal level... he flatly refused to engage in any public activity or to write in Spanish, the only language permitted at the time ... He had decided his world had been destroyed by the war... He deliberately sought out the kingdom of death, the negation of the life which lay before him."

Song of Silent Death

They ask: "Do you envy
your compatriots still able
to sing their songs?
The rest surrender
to this lethal hush.
Humbly we adore
our death."

Clock: rose, sand,
rose, desert. And then?
Just the deep down dread of someone
ousted, anonymous, alert
to the showy, departing sun.

Night's battlements: at times
a rustling of wings
in the atmosphere,
an already imprisoned dream.
I lumber along, fiercely pursued
by my own snowy footprints.

And I feel how the mute
death of men whisks away
my gift of words:
my pain
becomes pure silence.

Sinera Cemetery

Goodbye to deceivers
insisting they'll negotiate
the torrent. They've taken
scissors to the flowers,
and wings, memories, glances,
my entire sea slows to a stop.
A tranquil night breeze wafts
over a glittering fountain, fire's
secret voices. In the staunch
hush of the ennobling trees
I prize so deeply, I travel
toward oblivion, trailing
loves, sailboats,
my dogged footsteps' final
doleful traces.

*

I first became riveted by Salvador Espriu's poetry through reading David H. Rosenthal's anthology, *Modern Catalan Poetry*. In New York City, I met the late David Rosenthal (1945-1992), a noted jazz critic and the foremost translator of Catalan literature into English, after finding a pivotal article he'd penned in *The Village Voice* about the richness and variety of Catalan literature. David kindly gave me the names and addresses of Catalan writers, and when I arrived for the first time in Barcelona in the summer of 1983, I was able to meet a few prominent Catalan poets, including Francesc Parcerisas, Catalonia's current leading poet. After studying the writers in David's anthology, I became drawn to the work of Salvador Espriu, particularly his first book, *Sinera Cemetery*. From this poetic sequence, I felt a keen sense of Arenys de Mar, his native town (referred to by the anagram Sinera in his diligently built literary world). I initially encountered Espriu's poetry in English, then Castilian, before making the decision to learn to read Catalan in order to translate his work, cutting methodically the many, still-joined Catalan pages, in the old style of publication, with a trusty penknife.

When I delved, with a newfound purpose, into Iberian history and discovered Franco's inglorious ban on the Catalan language, it appealed to my sense of justice, as an African American poet, to learn a persecuted language. Espriu was only 23 when the civil war ignited. As a literary prodigy myself (in America I won the National Poetry Series at age 23), it was a daunting stretch for me to imagine my language and publication possibilities utterly stripped away. Studying Espriu's austere work and hieratic life, translating Catalan poetry, fiction, and plays became an integral part of my moral and political education abroad. Like most Americans, I had no clue that there were four languages in Spain (called *Sepharad* in Espriu's work, paralleling the Israelites' desert exile and Franco's harsh dictatorship, as Sephardic Jews were expelled or forced to convert by Ferdinand and Isabella's 15th century decree), and had no clue to the savage, complex dynamics of the Spanish Civil War and the long-lasting crucible of Franco's *(El Caudillo's)* repressive reign:

> Sometimes it's essential, even ordained
> that a man should die for a people,
> but a whole people must never perish
> for one man alone:
> remember this always, Sepharad.
> Make the bridges of dialogue iron-strong
> and do your utmost to foster
> your children's diverse minds and tongues. . .

> (from *The Bull's Hide*, XLVI,)

*

In an essay published in *Writing: A Mosaic of New Perspectives*, poet-translator Randall Couch depicts the process of translation as a burning house: "A poem to be translated is a house, if not a palace, on fire. It contains diverse occupants to be carried over (*translatio*) to safety in another place. The fire exists because of the incommensurability of languages, and its intensity ensures that, at least in the first instance, the act of translation will result in loss. So the question 'To what, or to whom, must the translator be faithful?' can be dramatized as 'What, or who, can be saved?' Couch quotes Cocteau's 'If my house was on fire, what would I take? / I'd like to take the fire.'"

Lisa Russ Spaar, in reviewing *Still Life with Children: Selected Poems of Francesc Parcerisas*, my translations of the Catalan poet, emphasizes translations as restoration, resurrection, renewal: "In many ways, a translation is a 'second act.' Survivors of house fires, for instance, will not only recount what they've been able to save from a burning building — a child, a pet, photographs, a piece of family jewelry, the clothes on their backs, a beloved book — but often speak as well of having been given a second chance, the gracious opportunity of starting anew."

Literary critic and Stanford Professor John Felstiner in his book, *Finding Neruda*, which focuses on his years of translating the great Chilean Nobel Laureate Pablo Neruda, also addresses the complex acrobatics, the champion feat achieved by dynamic translations: "Bring over a poem's ideas, and you will lose its manner; imitate its prosodic effects, and you will sacrifice its matter. Get the letter and you miss the spirit, which is everything in poetry; or get the spirit and you miss the letter, which is everything in poetry. But these are false dilemmas... Verse translation, at its best, generates a whole new utterance in a second language, new yet equivalent, of equal value."

My emphasis here in depicting my odyssey as a translator is on the "finding" process implied in Felstiner's title. Part of the work of a major translation project is education and discovery, initiation and immersion into the world of the poet; this can entail several things— in my case, learning to read a banned language, acquiring a political and moral education abroad, and a great mystical leap of faith.

Dogged revision and distillation over three and a half decades has been my process toward rendering what Dídac Llorens-Cubedo calls Espriu's "gravely meditative but intensely lyrical poetry." In the post-war era, when Espriu was deeply aggrieved about the survival of the Catalan language, in the face of such relentless repression and bullying, each word in Catalan became utterly precious to the poet. As a result, in translating his work, I have aimed to give weight and consideration to each word, to convey that sense of sacramental, ruby-like purity. Rather than an absolutely direct translation, I have favored crafting versions that sound and work artfully as poems in English. I have received major inspiration from my dear friend and colleague Magda Bogin's impressive translations of Espriu, which were published by Norton in 1989 and have remained consistently in print.

There's a powerful transmission of silence, both cruelly imposed and natural, in Espriu's flinty work. In his terse, fine-crafted "Dawn Song," there's a sense of imminent danger and potential violence, that arrives quickly and powerfully at the end:

Dawn Song

Wake to the newborn day,
the mounting sun's light,
old Virgil
ushering you
through hushed, smoky roads.
Leave nothing
till sundown,
save traveling and witness,
for, in a moment's flash,
everything will become seized prey.

The juxtaposition of the "mounting" sun as an emblem of hope and aspiration with the image of "seized prey" makes this a beautifully tensile poem—one with a striking, haiku-like swiftness, profundity, and concision. It's not difficult to read into the imagery a trace of Espriu's dismay and weariness at a world so prone to strife, attack, and bloodshed. In translating the spare, burnished quality of the original, I aimed for a pertinent musicality and transparent beauty in English, with the last word of the first line and last word of the last line rhyming: "day" and "prey," and a repetition of certain sounds, such as "ushered," "hush," and "flash." To highlight the swooping quality and surprise of the last line, I used much shorter, delicate lines to precede it.

In my own translations, I decided to focus on Espriu's succinct evocation and keenly conveyed sense of the land—which comes through potently in the early work, rather than focusing and rendering later poems, which are often intently psychological or oracular:

During the long summer we've witnessed
many wild fires
in our old, almost treeless country.
When the sun plummeted behind hills,
dusk burst into flames
that slowly opened
desolate night's wide doors.
The wind whirls and circles
from the south or southwest:
in the fields, always, always,
the wind's dry breath.
The drought stanches streams,
razes crops, drives
the sound of rain into memory
in vineyards, creeks,
and the sea's pathways...

(from "Possible Introduction to an Epithalamium")

My initial visit to the spellbinding hilltop cemetery in Arenys de Mar, the sanctuary and setting of Espriu's first poetry book, was indeed one of the most compelling events of my ongoing odyssey as a translator; my return to the sublime, panoramic site, where the writer is now buried in a simple, white columbarium, was the dynamic completion, for my part, of a profound emotional and spiritual arc. The cemetery's front wall now bears the final lines of Espriu's gravely beautiful first book, and this was immensely moving to witness. Seeing a somewhat weathered, clandestine first edition of *Sinera Cemetery* in the center for the study of Espriu's work *(Centre Espriu Arenys,* formerly *Centre d'Estudis i Documentació Salvador Espriu),* run by stalwart Montserrat Caba, was also an inspiring, poignant high point in my process of rendering this able, meticulous flame-keeper into English.

To fashion this unusual tribute, I have translated Espriu's first volume of poetry, *Sinera Cemetery* (originally published underground in 1946) and complementary selections from several of his other volumes. I must say that translating Espriu's complex work has indeed enhanced my own development as a poet (especially in terms of heightened linguistic sensitivity and dexterity) and spurred me toward the theme of spiritual endurance, the main focus of my second book, *Soul Make a Path through Shouting.*

As the final movement in my tribute, I have presented three poems of my own, written over a period of thirty years: "To The Cypress Again and Again," "Two Poets Quarreling under the Jacarandas" (inspired by Espriu's legendary friendship with the young Mallorcan poet, Bartolomeu Rosselló-Pòrcel) and "More Than Peace and Cypresses." The photos are from a summer pilgrimage I took with the great Barcelona-based poet Francesc Parcerisas to the cemetery in Arenys de Mar.

*

My experience as a translator is the most dramatic one I know. In the summer of 1984, I shared my Espriu translations with my friend and mentor, H. Joan Freeman, a deeply intuitive and highly regarded astrologer and columnist. She called me, on a dog day evening on Cape Cod, to say she needed to discuss my translations in person, adding, "don't worry, they're beautiful." When I arrived at her bay-facing, A-frame house in Provincetown, she informed me that, while reading Espriu's work, it became bell-clear to her "that this man's about to die and you must do everything in your power to see him before he goes. You must leave for Spain as soon as you can." Fortunately, I was in a position to travel again to Barcelona. Time never ticked so loudly for me as the warm September I waited to secure a meeting with the high priest of Catalan letters.

Through generous and thoughtful friends, it was arranged for me to stay with writer and director Guillem-Jordi Graells, a key figure of the Catalan National Theater—a boon, since Jordi had a fantastic library of Catalan literature that included all of Espriu's works. In the final days of my month-long stay, I finally revealed Joan's unsettling prophecy about Espriu's imminent death to Alèx Susanna, a friend and poet my age, who was translating T.S. Eliot's *Four Quartets* into Catalan! A few days later, in a café, Alèx announced: "we are going to meet Espriu!" He had arranged, through the Mallorcan poet, Jaume Vidal Alcover (1923-1991), a longtime friend of Espriu, for a visit to the poet's elegant place on the Passeig de Gràcia, so that I could submit my translations to Espriu directly. Given the fact that he was notoriously private and reclusive, Alèx and I expected the meeting to be relatively brief and formal. To our astonishment, we stayed for four hours and were joined by the great Catalan novelist, Maria Aurèlia Capmany, Alcover's partner, who brought along a scrumptious box of chocolates.

It was the first week of October 1984, in the days that preceded the annual announcement of the Nobel Prize for Literature, and in a drape of cigar smoke, Alcover and Capmany reminded Espriu that he was Catalan Spain's prime candidate; Espriu shook his head, insisting that the Nobel jurors were loathe to give the prize to a writer working in a stateless language. The revered literary critic Harold Bloom once hailed Espriu as "an extraordinary poet by any international standard," and later insisted, "The Nobel committee is guilty of many errors, and one of those was not to have given the prize to Salvador Espriu. I believe he deserved it."

During our surprising visit, Espriu expressed disbelief that I had never read Cervantes's *Don Quixote*, then granted me written permission for my versions, kindly promising to respond to my labor. As he signed the permission, he mentioned that he felt the finest translations of his work were in English. Alèx and I left our unexpectedly vibrant, even buoyant evening with Espriu and his longtime friends, all extraordinary writers, as if we two up-and-coming poets had been to visit the fabled Wizard of Oz.

The day after Espriu's death on February 22, 1985, Alèx received, in haunting fashion, a package from Espriu, meticulously wrapped, with a signed volume of his poetry. Alèx let Maria Aurèlia Capmany and Jaume Alcover know of my mentor Joan Freeman's unerring prophecy of Espriu's death, and they were naturally stunned. As fate would have it, Espriu died the same weekend as my paternal grandfather, and it was all so extraordinary, mysterious, and overwhelming a series of events and coincidences, that, despite continuing to refine my Espriu translations, I didn't return to Barcelona for twenty years!

So here, dear reader, is the long-in-coming result of my profound and truly mystical journey into Catalan literature and culture. From the start of my project, I was seeking to create something personal, almost indescribable, about my uncanny encounter with so venerable a man and writer. As a now mature artist, I like to imagine myself a diligent, cosmopolitan heir to immensely purposeful and devoted Espriu: an intrepid African American writer and ambassador working frankly and fearlessly in the world-at-large. As my brilliant friend, the Paris-based American poet Ellen Hinsey once asserted, "poetry is an independent ambassador for conscience: it answers to no one, it crosses borders without a passport, and it speaks the truth." Certainly the master-builder Espriu's impactful and absorbing work reached me, at the start of my own burgeoning career, in such a powerful and borderless way.

Cyrus Cassells, San Francisco, April 8, 2020

CEMENTIRI DE SINERA

POEMA ÚLTIM

QUAN ET DETURIS
ON EL MEU NOM ET CRIDA,
VULGUES QUE DORMI
SOMNIANT MARS EN CALMA,
LA CLAROR DE SINERA.

SALVADOR ESPRIU

*II. BECAUSE ONE DAY THE SONG WILL RETURN
TO SINERA: A SAMPLER OF ESPRIU'S POETRY*

BLACK LAND

Rest, linger on your journey: look,
under the sun's gold-flooded eye,
a limitless kingdom.
The lulled breeze dozes
on a placid, solitary plain.

Upriver, passing between parallel
desert walls, a god's vessel nears.
A thousand dazzling flags
flutter on its sun-struck masts.
Rowing priests chant antediluvian hymns
to death's master, as their oars
strike mud, swelling waves.

This light, this livelong day's tranquility
are yours, traveler, if the vast earth
of unending wheat
cries out your name.

BOOK OF THE DEAD

Mark how you'll progress,
stripped of wisdom,
along the weatherworn road
only once,
till suddenly an oracle
will trumpet the kept-secret name
assigned to you
at your death.
Warning: there's no turning back.
Make sure never to stray
from what's easiest to love:
wheat fields, home's specter,
a boat's white speck
bobbing at sea,
unambitious winter's gold
languishing in the vineyards,
a tree's shadow unfurled
across a spacious field.
Oh, please revere, above all else,
that hallowing tree's vitality:
the bountiful, invisible wind roaring
through sun-gilded branches.

SINERA CEMETERY

I

Down stream-paths coursing
through vine-and-fennel-laden hills,
the leave-taking sun's chariot sweeps—
through hills, so unforgettable.
I'll pass through a hall
of cypresses,
so green, immobile above
the hushed sea.

II

Behold how my little homeland
surrounds Sinera Cemetery.
Pine-and-vineyard-adorned hills,
the immense sea,
the dust of dried-up streams.
I love nothing, save
a cloud's migrant shadow.
The slow memories of days
lost forever.

III

Bereft of names and symbols,
beside the mourning trees,
beneath a tidbit of sandy,
rain-stiffened dirt.
Let the wind scatter
ash in boats
and fine-drawn furrows,
marring Sinera's
April clarity,
my homeland's light
perishing with me,
as I ponder the years,
all that's passed:
arduous trek to slow twilights'
terminus.

IV

Already my eyes can do little
save ponder years and suns
gone by. I can still hear
old carriages wheeling
through Sinera's insolvent streams!
From memory
come the smells of a sea
watched over by radiant summers.
The rose I once picked
still lingers on my fingertips.
And on my lips,
wind, fire, words already
relegated to ash.

V

Mendicant of old memories,
I knock at every door,
as my futile prayer
resounds through Sinera's streets.
No charity can restore
yesterday's satisfying bread,
castaway time. In green solitude,
unfailing cypresses wait
to give me alms.

VI

Spiders spin
regal palaces,
rooms that snare
winter's footsteps.
Sinera's boats
no longer set sail,
for the old sea-routes
have vanished.
The sun can't decorate the ice
with festive damasks
for a sightless pilgrim.
Tiny bells no longer
ring from Sinera's stream beds.
Again, I pass between rows
of cypresses.

VII

Tender grapes come,
courtesy of a bestowing martyr's
silver hand.
Miniature lights
of processional candles tremble
and spur afternoon's
last rites: viaticum
of Sinera's kaleidoscopic memories;
to muse on them, I climb
to a presiding cypress.
Moonlight kisses
a hierarchy of peaks.

VIII

Surely rain's coming,
for the peak nicknamed
"Grandmother Muntala"
has stashed the sun in her armoire
of gusty weather,
among her lacy
mantilla of storm clouds, woven
by Sinera's tiny fingers.
Some bird craves to penetrate Muntala's
prison-cage of light. I ponder
serene cypresses in the wide
garden of my silence.
By the sea's everlasting hem
dolphins pass.

IX

In the delicate, drifting harmony
that results from the downpour
and the laggard afternoon,
fleeting memories of rain
deepen the wilting flowers' ordeal.
How hushed the sea's become!
And high above it,
Sinera's embattled kingdom, trapped
in a sharp-pointed siege:
See, the sentinel cypresses have culled
the sky's bright weeping
as brief mirrors.

X

The arranger of rows
of doleful trees and silence, I confer
a magic scepter's serene authority
into trustworthy hands.
Night, wind, hymn,
ancient bronze forged against
the rain's army,
a harsh solitude confronted
time and again.
Shepherding gods nudge clouds
in docile flocks
to the sierra.

XI

The rain dies
and becomes its own mirror.

Flickering lights lure
    lingering moths.

A night wind dozes
in the fields, in the cemetery.

When it reawakens,
    it will be a new day.

XII

Boxwood and a chaste-tree
in an ilex's shade.
Each morning
their leaves shiver
as the reviving wind
surges from the fields.

XIII

Lazing clouds leave shadows
on white cemetery walls
immuring mid-day's
fathomless silence.

XIV

Crystal-pure memory,
the murmur of fountains, of clear,
ebbing voices.
With dreamy, gilded pauses,
I pass the long afternoon.

XV

In local salt marshes,
the cold slow sound
of resounding bells.
Mist and crickets lord
all the afternoon paths.

XVI

Docile-eyed guards go by,
cordoning off Sinera's memory.
Night is at its peak,
igniting tranquil messages
of flourishing life
beyond the graveyard's margins.

XVII

O black boat
that docked during my night-vigil,

black boat sailing through my reverie
of Sinera's sea!

Now a woman's timeless voice
allows me to detect

a hymn of marble.

XVIII

The boat anchors
in Sinera's peace,
where ancient hands rest
        under ancient trees.

A close-by vineyard's fire
signals summer's end,
as in solitude I await
the errant hours.

XIX

The ostiaries
of an ancient cult open
doorways to the dance
of the sinner and the saint,
amid horses dashing from the sea,
reined to chariots
of black weather.

The wind broadcasts fall smoke
on fine marble altars,
on gold-thick vineyards,
darkening the face
of each pilgrim who undertakes
the cypress path.

XX

Maple and holly,
secret snow,
the bedeviling *tramuntana's*
thin, chilly air.
Seaside winter: a fragile sun
above deserted beaches.

XXI

Wild, dawn-burnished horses
dot a deserted beach.
Drums and voices herald
                spring's nativity.

Later, at the shoreline,
ensuing silence:
chained hours kiss
            wet sands.

XXII

On wet sand
I preserve the balance
of an architectural order.

Subtle, deeply devout,
and utterly daunted
by dogma,
I wrestle with
singular thoughts
along cold, rain-washed
metaphysical roads.

My splintered voice becomes
the crystal of my pain—
Sundays and tomorrows
the same, always the same,
as the April light dies,
and I struggle to prevent
the vaulted sky from falling.

XXIII

As the April light died,
and the singing daughters
were silenced,
in twilight's hush,
I paced the rooms
of my lost house.

XXIV

No elegiac waves
will be carved from marble,
nor soaring angels' flights
from envisioned empires,
for, lightning-quick, harsh weather
is here. Memory's voices impel me
through Sinera's tenantless rooms,
to the dawn's watchman:
a cypress familiar
with on-fire clouds and seas.

XXV

By the sea, I had
a house, my slow dream.
By the sea.

High prow. Along the water's
freest pathways, the fragile
boat I captained.

My eyes relished
all my small land's
serenity and poise.

Raindrops on my windowpane
deepen my fear.
Now night engulfs my house.

Black rocks lure me
toward shipwreck.
Prisoner of my own singing,

all my efforts futile,
who can steer me
toward dawn?

By the sea, I had
a house,
a slow dream.

XXVI

I can't struggle any longer.
I leave you this vast
sepulcher that was once
our fathers' land:
dreams, meanings.
I'm dying,
since I can't gauge
how to live.

XXVII

Dreams, meanings, vivid
boats in the wind,
liberty, the enduring word I utter
time and again,
between ancient boundaries
of vineyards and the sea.
I don't rally myself
to the task of living,
for I don't know how.
White walls surround me,
the grieving trees'
benevolent, towering peace,
beneath dust and shadow.

XXVIII

This peace is my possession
and God remains my beacon.
I utter to the root, the cloud:
"This peace is mine."

From my garden I mark
how slowly the hours pass
before my opaque eyes.
And God is my beacon.

XXIX

The footsteps of a longtime friend
who still contemplates
a far-off, impossible God:
Are you seeking some name
to stop you?

And with this holy name,
will you learn
the ultimate secret
of all who've lived before you?
Such a lonely man.

XXX

When you halt suddenly,
there where my name
haunts you,
wish me a profound dream
of tranquil seas
and Sinera's splendor.

B., March 1944-May 1945

SONG OF TWILIGHT

after Sebastia, Francesc, and Isabel went to play
on the mountain called Bad Weather

Before my very eyes, children's voices whisked away
the sun I was accustomed to seeing.
So much summer light
spurred me to dreaming.

A clock on a white wall announces
the ebbing afternoon.
A docile wind is vanishing
on dusk-lit roads.

Maybe tomorrow a slow,
durable brightness
will act as balm
to my burning gaze.

But now it is night,
and I linger alone
in the house of the dead,
whom only I recall.

from BECAUSE ONE DAY THE SONG WILL RETURN
TO SINERA

My long-deterred dream
of an immense white peace
beneath a clement sky.

I travel laconic roads
that reward me
with shimmering peaks.

Time is stopped
in these lofty
headland vineyards;

I myself have stopped it,
guarding my treasured memories
from harridan winter...

In an eerie void,
they mounted this silence
and this solitude.

They barely remain names:
tree, house, earth,
plough-land, furrow, woman.

Only the fragile words
of my language,
root and seed.

The sea, the old pine,
the augured boat.
The fear of death.

MEMORY

Always I hear
your eternal silence
on the mountain.
Other times, other hours
make remembering difficult.

FROM THE THEATER ITSELF

I know, even now, in my memory,
the smile's intact.
But the hands, already gone
to ash or light,
where, where will I find them again?

AUTUMN

The wind and the woods die
as they kiss
the afternoon's sullen light.
Nighttime legions advance
along solitary roads.

THE GARDEN OF FIVE TREES

Later when I'd already caused myself
ample pain,
and the most I could muster
was a smile,
I opted for the simplest
words to tell myself
how the sun's rays
slowly traveled the lavish ivy
in the garden of five trees.
In the fugitive yellow
of a winter sunset,
the last winding fingers of water
plummeted from lofty clouds,
and the cross weather cast my soul
deep into dungeons of silence.

from *THE BOOK OF SINERA*

(I)

Ultra-slow, unending,
beyond Time's ceaseless unfolding,
listen to the hard-knocking hoe,
past the hedge and high wall.

They've uprooted vines, burned shoots,
building a wilderness of the exalted earth.
Alongside the sinuous stream-path, we shuffle,
with weary, anxious feet.

Fallow fields, brittle, windswept reeds
trumpet their wisdom:
"Behold yourself in us, as you claim
your allotted death."

Hunched in shadow, hired hands
hoe winter's stripped-away vines.
In the vast, dull sky, there's no detectable light,
just the knocking hoe's tattoo in deepening winter.

from THE BOOK OF SINERA

(II)

You're winter-settled,
and the brisk earth,
roused by a hoe
and hauled, bit by bit,
from hollows, spreads
and peppers the flagging wall
with a scattering of snails'
little desiccated shells.
Ah, such small aims
already stripped of sense,
forever distant from priceless chalices
that hold the rights to sleep
and the master's mockery!
Nevertheless, a shoal of fish roils
the darkened sea,
where I know, to my core,
the deep trench and cove,
and the wind's breath stirs
the fallow field, distilling
on slim fennel,
a delicate film of remembered mist.

from *END OF THE LABYRINTH*

(XI)

Hunter, immersed in dawn's mist,
what do you see,
what do you see now:
a man, a deer, a tree?
Keep your dead-sure lance,
your masterly arrow. You'll pierce
more thoroughly
the secret of this lonely,
utterly lucid life,
if you wound it
with a well-honed axe.
But watch me first,
beyond this waking hour's
tranquility.
Guess what I am
at the water's edge.

SONG OF TRIUMPHANT NIGHT

Where the gold slowly ends,
flags, unfurling night.

Listen to the roar
of countless waters
and a wind opposing you:
unbridled horses.

When you hear the hunter's horn,
its bold blast,
you'll be summoned forever
to surrender to dusk's kingdom.

An ancient, deep-rooted pain
that has never known dawn!

OMNIS FORTASSE MORIAR

Blood-flecked dusk:
A veiled combat spurs
slow sundown's relinquished moan,
burnishing distant peaks:
From the well-bottoms
of a blind man's eyes, I've watched
the slandered mutt known as night
scuttle fear's wide paths,
broadcasting my demise
in enormous howls.
Tuneless bird, wordless wood,
fast-asleep prince, wind-gust!
Prediction: I'll reach my end,
anonymous, minus even a trace,
stripped of wounds or memories.
Ears attuned to
water's lucent voices,
the rustling leaves' exodus,
and the last heart.
Bit by bit, I'll become
family: a burgeoning
brother to lowly mud.

WINTER JOURNEY

Storm clouds keep harassing
God's fortress,
but I respond with silence,
since the era of words
has come to a jagged close.

I smile at the onerous message
of those long-trammeled hours.
What I know, in my embattled soul:
a civil war's slaughter
obliterated my world.

In desolate winter, at night
I trudge past the sea's stiff plain,
powerless to locate
hope's island, its latitude.
Deep in my marrow, what I understand:
bloodshed and strife
annihilated my treasured world.

OFFERING TO CERBERUS

I've dedicated my whole life to words,
chewed this mongrel's morsel
into a long-lasting meal.
Have mercy, sentry,
on my frail bones and feeble skeleton,
for I arrive, sans
a single scrap of flesh!
I submerge my outcast's hands
into my precious Catalan's
mysterious gold and present them,
profitless, white with ash
from a fire I kindled myself,
as the brittle sound of fragile glass
dwindles in the abyss
under my lids.
I dance, in wincing pain,
to earn the crowd's sneers and chuckles,
its brusque applause,
and, at the burlesque's close,
I'm crowned with a jester's cap.

THE WAITING

Then I'll sing: "Summits, clouds,
and distant countries, a river's
deepening gash, blazing skies
of numerous desert twilights,
and longstanding trees
venerated like gods—yes, they all return
to humanity.
But I, who awaited this day,
here I am, already dead."

FELT IN THE STYLE OF SALVADOR ESPRIU

I'll have to pay my old price, death,
and the light today exhausts my eyes.
Unnerved, I've descended countless steps
and plunged into midnight's sunless realm.

Immersed in silence, I rise as night's sovereign,
yet envision myself an apprentice to anyone who knows grief.
But how do I lead such limitless sorrow
to the sanctum of night's language?

The wind passes through a phalanx of flames and archers:
so does victory and tantalizing sleep.
Prisoner of my dead, captive of my own name,
trudging alone, I'm transformed into a wall.

Derailed by fear, far from maps, messages,
and music, I'm one of the forsaken.
My lament, just the dark dream of someone
ousted from the palaces of light.

TREE

I dreamt your invisible majesty
looming near the old name
of each thing.
Rooted in ash-thick grief,
merely a man, I shouldered you,
soundlessly, within me,
sepulcher, dead father,
and ambushed you with windswept words
of ancient millennia, words
mighty enough to incite fury.
But you've never responded
to all my clamoring,
and consign me to my deepest
nighttime fears,
secret fire, upraised flame,
god-tall titan in the dark.

from THE BOOK OF SINERA

(L)

Despite everything, the sturdy pine-tree
roots in terrific dryness,
and leans into a liberating breeze,
wind I name and emblazon
with the letters of a fleeting,
innately noble,
and time-defiant word:
I lift my hoary trunk
above the ancient,
still-enduring sea,
shading and sheltering,
with a watchman's aegis,
my well-worn path.
Night's placater, I permit
light's persistent clarity
to rest in me,
while I turn my rugged voice
into an austere tor of song.

TRIAL HYMN IN THE TEMPLE

Oh, how fed up I've become
with my brute, puny homeland,
and how I'd fancy a getaway up north,
where the citizens, rumor has it,
are learned, noble-hearted,
well-heeled, wide-awake,
spotless, carefree,
and oh-so-full of spirit.
But, in the congregation,
the disapproving elders
would undoubtedly lament:
Like a bird veering from the nest
is he who forsakes his home-place,
while, far away, I'd chuckle
at the stodgy rules and ancient logic
of my stick-in-the-mud village.
But that dream of joyous exodus
can't be pursued,
and I'll languish here
till my final breath,
for I'm fearful and bumbling too,
and above all, love,
with a go-for-broke grief,
my downcast, pitiful,
and far from lucky homeland.

AFTER THE TREES

When I can no longer lose myself
in lush snow, an acolyte
of lights and clashing horizons
looming above
my country's imperiled trees,
I'll know the wanderer's bone-deep weariness
for the bonanza
of a home-place and fountain,
exhilarating smells of earth
and sliced bread set on the table.
Then, unchained at last
from fear and hope,
I'll lull myself to sleep forever,
listening to the slow
sound of hoes in broad fields,
the rustle of dusk
among the vine-tendrils.

III. FOR THE CATALAN KEEPER OF THE FLAME:
POEMS INSPIRED BY SALVADOR ESPRIU

TO THE CYPRESS AGAIN AND AGAIN

in memory of Salvador Espriu
(1913-1985)

Sinera (Arenys de Mar, Spain)

I woke to ash in my mouth:
Don't bark! Speak the language of the Empire!

Everywhere silence, dispiriting silence.
Old men fined on the streets;
Children whipped
For a single word:

It was like the dream of Joseph in Egypt,
The dream in the dungeon, the dank well,
Or the plangent cry of Job,
The fortunate man who wakes in hell,
Tested by a fire from heaven—

*

Beside the cypress, for a while I could believe
God was not dead—
Under the first avid stars;
He had spared my country:
In light and shadow, in merciful beauty,
My village arrayed,
And beneath the yoke of solitude,
A distant majesty of dolphins—

*

In those ardent days of the Republic,
Years of shared bread,
My language filled me
Like heady wine,
Laced with a sweetness of figs,
The tang of pine nuts—my country
An almond tree in bloom,
The Mediterranean my garden—
Blue, voluminous—

But then came armies of the dead—

Sometimes I'd sit before the blank, impoverished page,
Till the rising sun reclaimed
Hills of vines and fennel,
And from wide fields would come
Voices of peasants,
Mingling with voices of my dead,
The sound of hoes striking my heart—

Always I was seeking
Something more than Cervantes.
More than the brutal pantomime of war.
More than the brunt of the black boot.
More than sin or the minotaur.
More, more than the fear of death—

An alphabet of cypresses and sea-light.

*

Cassells,
The name could be Mallorcan—

How old are you?:

Twenty-seven,
And you've never read *Don Quixote*!

*

To the cypress, to the scintillant blue
Dress of the Mediterranean
Swishing off to the Balearics,
Year after year, you climbed,
To the cemetery with its hush of marble—
Your language like sweetly-guarded seeds
In your breastpocket:

At any moment
You could have tossed them to the wind—

I reached your village:
How the cemetery crowns Sinera!
The wind ushered me to
Your corridor of cypress:
Wondrous trees that listen
And answer back.
So I asked for the hard word you cherished
Between ancient boundaries
Of vineyards and sea.

Like gods, in green unison, the cypress let go
In lucent whisper:

Liberty.

*

Bring me all the adjectives of the rock—
Adamant, tenacious, obstinate, unwavering—
For Salvador Espriu is dead—

You slipped away from me
So quickly, Espriu,
Yet blessed me
With the subtlest gift:

The wealth and mystery of our single meeting—

*

It was beyond the Pyrenees, in Perpignan,
That I saw it for the first time:
Families streaming from their tables to begin
The *sardana*, your native dance,
Banned for many years,
A deft, living circle
Mirroring sunrise—
The light, a dawn of hands
Linked in deep Mediterranean laughter.

*

Cyrus, when Franco died, the champagne vanished
From all the hoary shelves of Sinera.
I held a glass to my lips—
The taste was keen, unimaginably kind—
And I called to my missing, my dead, to return
From the manacled kingdoms of exile.
Then I climbed to my battlement of lush trees.

(1986)

TWO POETS QUARRELING UNDER THE JACARANDAS

I. The Quarrel

The Big Dipper spilling into a grammar
of almonds and valley wind,
muscatel and bougainvillea—
Near the lordly bell tower,
under the polestar rovers,
we were quarreling in the path
of billowing jacarandas—blue-violet shreds
italicizing the town walkways
under our moonlit sandals.
Half-drunk, en route to the hill
of the hard-at-work windmill,
dear ghost, tell me, what were we
at loggerheads about?
So help me, I can't recall—

Out of love, I'd come
to marvel at a Mediterranean Oz
of innumerable lemon rows,
to reach your family's finca
at the *tramuntana's* hem,
where Flor, your mother, revealed
an infallible, carved eagle,
forever guarding your filigreed cradle—

That clashing moment
under the giveaway branches,
when your mutinous bangs erupted
over your brows,
your expressive mind racing past
your prepossessing body—
your suddenly unruly hair,

turned almost caution yellow
in moonlight and lamplight,
why is that the singular moment
I can't relinquish?
That's as real and vital to me now
as my gnarled hand
holding up a morning glory
in your boyhood garden,
fifty years after the revolution and civil war—

II. Carnival of Fire

Hard to believe, after half a century,
I'm here, relishing your Mallorcan home,
ensconced under another unbridled,
shedding, May-time jacaranda—
My able doctors insist I'm dying,
but what's death
after the doleful exodus of so many souls
during and following the civil war?
Your last surviving sister, Maria del Sol,
still witty and perceptive,
still unfettered in her approach
to Catalan life and politics,
not in the least provincial,
embraced me at the wrought-iron gate
but at supper, she whispered, slyly:

Batman and Robin,
Estragon and Vladimir,
Sancho and Quixote:
Half the island debated
if it was love, the pants-off kind!,
she laughed, *or merely friendship—*

So I ping-ponged back:
Mari, what do you believe?

I have my theories.
Wasn't it passion that turned you
into a poet?
An even greater one than him.
That had to be my brother's doing.
Possession almost!

I didn't answer your testing,
never-taciturn sister;
in mischief's name, she didn't expect,
much less require an answer;
I know, beneath it all, Maria was itching to ask:
Why did you lie and pretend
you visited him in the sanitarium,
when I know otherwise?
But even for her, there are limits
to her X-ray frankness—

So, as ever, I carried on, safeguarding
our youthful link, our secrets,
then segued into the lissome garden,
where, in lieu of your impassioned voice,
proclaiming, at the war's outset,
rage and bigotry
brought us to this bloodshed,
I heard heartening bells emit
from the mountain monastery,
the sound of cormorants' cries,
while the valedictory sun and headland sky
became an ecstatic carnival of fire.

III. Torch-Pass

Did your death stop my singing?
It did. For a dozen years, it's true,
no public performances
(underworld, chrysalis, total eclipse),
then I had Francesc and Lluc Maria fashion
fitting music for your poems—
the earliest ones evoking
port-of-call nets, pine-laden summits,
fields of shimmering olive and citrus,
and Lord, I was impelled, all systems go,
to sing again.
The infernal vortex, the battle between brothers
was a memory,
and marauding Franco's irascible ban
against our sacramental language
(Don't bark! Speak the language of the empire!)
began to loosen a little.
No, it wasn't adequate
to broadcast your captivating words
before a reverent crowd,
to eulogize your genius
in a candlelit island chapel
or a Valencia concert hall;
I was gripped by a galvanizing desire
to compose poetry as well.
A tenor and storytelling prodigy,
yet I'd never fashioned a single stanza
in the time preceding the war,
but after your upending death,
every word of our denigrated language
became precious ore;
in this torch-pass, I let go
interpreting *bel canto* and perfecting stories:

I became all poetry,
all silence and verse—

IV. The Keats Mirror

What god would make a Keats
and subtract his breath?
That's what you lamented
when we made our avid pilgrimage
to the "live-in-the-eye" poet's
narrow room, overlooking
the folderol of the Spanish Steps,
and when we gazed on the pauper's bed
where lamp-like John died
(at the very last, the prodigy's lungs
"completely destroyed,"
the whole flummoxed chamber
of his exhausted thorax
utterly blackened)—
we were mercifully undone and lucky
to mourn in peace for awhile—

Then, worshipful students,
unflagging fans, we bought Parma violets
for the gone-too-soon poet's
innately humble grave,
beside the stone of his loyal helpmate,
Joseph Severn.
There in the lulling corner
near the cat-loved pyramid of Caius Cestius,
in the Protestant Cemetery, we overheard
a little towheaded schoolboy ask,
And where is Mr. Keats?
In heaven?
And his fanciful mother answered:
I imagine he's on Hampstead Heath, son;
I imagine he's busy being a bee
or a nightingale—

In that Roman place of tranquil,
sun-reaching cypresses,
you shared the endearing tale
of a blissfully truant shepherd
that stalwart Severn once spied
dozing against the poet's grave—

And from the lofty but regretful
crow's nest of old age
and impending death
(Why do we love and fail?
Why are we meant to live and feel
the myriad ways we die?)
now I realize: you were my own
confounding Keats, my heart's crash
(who could have forecast
you'd suffer the nightingale poet's,
the writ-in-water dreamer's fate?),
but I was no wartime Severn
by your bedside—

V. The Hill of Muses

With our small coterie of dreaming-out-loud
scholars and writers,
we quit prodigal Rome and blatant Naples
for fabled Greece.
Though web-spinning Hitler, that master builder,
had wheedled his way to power
the previous winter,
on that intoxicating summer jaunt,
our own portable student world seemed
beautiful, impregnable—

In a downpour, we realized,
on the final dusk of our Aegean tour,
we were adjacent to Socrates's jail
and the panoramic Hill of Muses,
with its vista-facing tomb
of the great Roman consul Philopappos,
and in your weather-marred hat
and soggy, cream-yellow linen,
amid the stern pines, the soft bodies
of short-lived cicadas, you laughed
at the coincidence, insisting:
tempests, Mussolini—it's a messy world,
but wherever there's laughter, Salvador,
there's freedom—

Word-sorcerer, the way you saw it,
as tenacious Greek and Latin pupils
(all of twenty, tanned and resourceful
as stranded Crusoe and Friday,
those foraging castaways),
we reached back to the pagan
to find a puissant syntax to describe

all we meant to each other:
jejune seekers, atavists, strays
from the classical world;
in timeless Greece, we didn't need to label
our clandestine touching
as trespass, apostasy, or a Judas goat,
only tradition—

VI. *Ashes and Jacarandas*

In the dire war aria that begins
the terrible news continues,
the doctors detected TB,
and, with greyhound alacrity, at Three Kings,
you were gone: even younger
than your cherished Keats—

Forgive me, in that downfall winter
of meager rations, reliable bombings,
mid-way through the impinging war,
I couldn't reach the sanitarium in time,
so I had to envision (till I believed
wholeheartedly in the fantasy)
the hovering nurses, the frowning doctor
with his chilly stethoscope,
the final, apocryphal embrace—
elegizing your unbearable passing
in mid-life verse, as if I had been there:
Lord help me, I wanted to be there,
to embrace you, yes—to hold even your urn
at the ash-gray end—

I lied, my poet, when I claimed
I couldn't pinpoint
the wellspring of our long-ago quarrel:
it was politics, of course, and more:
in the eleventh hour of the Republic,
in that engrossing chaos, that free-for-all
in which a man might be murdered
just for wearing a tie,
you'd urged us to flee the country,
and I had confessed, foolishly:
I couldn't imagine giving up Barcelona,
even for you…

In the island moonlight, you halted,
to emphasize your point;
your insurgent bangs cascaded
over your impressive forehead
and penetrating eyes,
then, all at once, you jettisoned
your fail-safe, wire-rimmed glasses,
and pulled my wary face to yours,
like a Roman or a Neapolitan!
Your near-kiss was the truce—
there, amid the frail firecracker shreds
of Mallorcan jacarandas,
where, in reverie or earnest prayer, I find,
as I move toward the dark frigate
of ever-demanding Death,
your point-blank beauty again…

(2017)

MORE THAN PEACE AND CYPRESSES

More than peace and cypresses, emboldened
hares at the field's edge,

Father, I love
gallantry, tenacity, the sanguine

heart before the ledge:
the artist questing and failing—

the feet of bested Icarus
plunging into the sea's crest—

the artist triumphing: a page of fire
from the book of heroes.

More than light-hooved gazelles, views
from the mizzenmast,

enlivening shores,
more than soldier-still lilies, I love

the torchlike men who've taught me—
past the rueful

glitter of lucre and guns,
past the starkness of the lynching tree—

the truth-or-bust beauty
of passion transformed

into sheer compassion,
true shouldering,

and common as breath, common as breath,
the extravagant wheel of birth and death.

(2003)

The portal of Sinera Cemetery (photo by Cyrus Cassells, 2018)

ABOUT THE WRITER

Salvador Espriu (1913-1985) was Catalan Spain's most venerated 20th century man of letters and its main contender for the Nobel Prize. After a sickly childhood in which Espriu was ill for two years, he began publishing short stories and novels during the early 1930's. During that same period he studied history and law, and was on the verge of taking a degree in classical languages when the Spanish Civil War erupted. He was then drafted into the army and served until 1939.

Espriu's first book of poetry, *Sinera Cemetery*, was published in an underground edition in 1946. Like many of his stories, it depicts the small village of Arenys de Mar (Sinera), his parents' hometown in the Costa del Maresme, a little north of Barcelona, where the poet had spent a fair amount of his youth.

Espriu's poetry wed political critique and denunciation with a brand of austere lyricism and often brooding, death-obsessed imagery, as the flame-keeping poet prevailed, despite Franco's long, truculent ban against the public use of Catalan. He fashioned a series of parallels between Jews and Catalans, whom Espriu felt were exiled from their collective identity even while they remained in their own land. 2013, the hundredth anniversary of his birth, was declared "The Year of Espriu" throughout Catalonia.

ABOUT THE TRANSLATOR

Cyrus Cassells, the 2021 Poet Laureate of Texas, is the author of nine books of poetry, including *Soul Make a Path through Shouting*, *The Gospel according to Wild Indigo*, and *The World That The Shooter Left Us*, (Four Way Books: 2022). He is the translator from Catalan of *Still Life with Children: Selected Poems of Francesc Parcerisas*, which garnered the Texas Institute of Letters' 2019 Souerette Diehl Fraser Award for Best Translated Book of 2018 and 2019. His honors include a Lannan Literary Award, a Lambda Literary Award, the National Poetry Series, an NAACP Image Award nomination, and the Poetry Society of America's William Carlos Williams Award. He is a tenured Professor of English at Texas State University, where he received the 2021 Presidential Excellence Award for Creative/Scholarly activities, one of the university's highest honors.

CPSIA information can be obtained
at www.ICGtesting.com
Printed in the USA
JSHW032227160223
37855JS00001B/8